student
WORKBOOK

OCR A2 Psychology
Unit G544: Approaches and Research Methods in Psychology
Molly Marshall

Philip Allan Updates, an imprint of Hodder Education, an Hachette UK company, Market Place, Deddington, Oxfordshire OX15 0SE

Orders

Bookpoint Ltd, 130 Milton Park, Abingdon, Oxfordshire OX14 4SB

tel: 01235 827827   fax: 01235 400401

e-mail: education@bookpoint.co.uk

Lines are open 9.00 a.m.–5.00 p.m., Monday to Saturday, with a 24-hour message answering service. You can also order through the Philip Allan Updates website: www.philipallan.co.uk

ISBN 978-1-4441-0850-7

© Philip Allan Updates 2010

First printed 2010

Impression number 5 4 3 2

Year 2013 2012 2011

Printed in Spain

Environmental information

Hachette UK's policy is to use papers that are natural, renewable and recyclable products and made from wood grown in sustainable forests. The logging and manufacturing processes are expected to conform to the environmental regulations of the country of origin.

Introduction

This workbook is designed to support your study of OCR A2 Unit G544: Approaches and Research Methods in Psychology. It focuses on what you need to learn in order to do well in the exam. Each topic looks at a different aspect of approaches and research methods, and the aim is to help you to increase your understanding and to improve your skills in answering the types of question that you might encounter in the exam.

You need to remember that G544 is a synoptic exam, but as there are four applied units (Forensic, Sport, Education and Health & Clinical) it is difficult to select/include material from the applied options that is appropriate for all students. In this workbook the research evidence has been drawn from the AS core studies, but the research you learn in applied units can and should also be drawn on, where appropriate, to illustrate your answers.

The workbook includes a variety of stimulus materials. The questions are wide-ranging and designed to support you as you develop skills of analysis, interpretation and evaluation. Writing answers to the questions will help you learn to communicate your knowledge and understanding of psychology in a clear and effective manner. As you complete the workbook, you should become confident that you are learning the content required for the exam and how to write answers that will achieve high marks.

The workbook is organised into two sections:
- In the first section on research methods, there are four topics:
  - Topic 1 focuses on how to identify, describe and evaluate the most frequently used research methods.
  - Topic 2 looks at the factors associated with research design, including techniques for improving validity and reliability.
  - Topic 3 examines data analysis and data presentation.
  - Topic 4 focuses on inferential statistics.
- In the second section on approaches, perspectives, issues and debates there are two topics:
  - Topic 1 focuses on psychological approaches and perspectives.
  - Topic 2 looks at issues and debates in psychology.

To gain maximum benefit, you should complete the questions on each topic in the order given. There are several ways in which you can use this workbook:
- As an integral part of your learning experience to be used in conjunction with your class notes, handouts and textbook. Periodically, your teacher might ask you to hand in your book for assessment.
- As a revision tool, in which case you should work through the topics, writing the answers as practice for the exam.
- As a combination of both. If, as you progress through the unit, you write answers to all the questions in this book, at the end of the course you will have created a valuable resource from which to revise.

Research methods

Topic 1 Research methods and techniques

Psychologists use many methods to conduct research. Each method has advantages and limitations, and the method selected needs to be appropriate for the topic of research:

- **Quantitative** research uses methods that measure amounts of behaviour, usually by assigning a numeric value to what is being measured (the quantity).
- **Qualitative** research measures what behaviour is like (the quality), and usually results in descriptive data.

In this topic, you will learn to identify, describe and evaluate the most frequently used research methodologies and designs.

Item 1 Experimental design

Laboratory experiments
A laboratory experiment is a method of conducting research in which researchers try to control all the variables except the one that is changed between the experimental conditions. The variable that is changed is called the **independent variable (IV)**, and the effect it may have is called the **dependent variable (DV)**. So the IV is manipulated, and its effect — the DV — is measured.

Strengths
- High levels of control in a laboratory experiment allow extraneous variables that might affect the IV or the DV to be minimised. The researcher can be sure that any changes in the DV are the result of changes in the IV.
- High levels of control make it possible to measure the effect of one variable on another. Statements about cause and effect can be made.
- Laboratory experiments can be replicated to check the findings with either the same or a different group of participants.

Limitations
- Laboratory experiments may not measure how people behave outside the laboratory in their everyday lives. Some experimental settings and tasks are contrived — thus the findings may have low internal validity.
- Aspects of the experiment may act as cues to behaviour that cause the participants (and the experimenter) to change the way they behave (demand characteristics), sometimes because of what they think is being investigated or how they think they are expected to behave. This can mean that it is not the effect of the IV that is measured, leading to invalid results.

Field experiments
A field experiment is a way of conducting research in an everyday environment, for example in a school or hospital, where one or more IVs are manipulated by the experimenter and the effect it may have (the DV) is measured.

One difference between laboratory and field experiments is an increase in the naturalness of the setting and a decrease in the level of control the experimenter is able to achieve. The key difference is the extent to which participants know they are being studied. In most field experiments, participants are not aware of being studied, which is why behaviour is more natural.

Strengths
- Field experiments allow psychologists to measure how people behave in their everyday lives. The findings may have high external validity.
- Manipulation of the IV and some level of control make it possible to measure the effect of one variable on another. Statements about cause and effect can be made.
- If participants do not know they are participating in a study, they will be unaware they are being watched or manipulated. It reduces the probability that their behaviour results from demand characteristics. However, this may not be true of all field experiments; the extent to which demand characteristics are present will vary depending on the experimental setting.

Limitations
- It is not always possible to control for extraneous variables that might affect the IV or the DV. The researcher cannot always be sure that any changes in the DV are the result of changes in the IV.
- Field experiments can be difficult to replicate, and thus it may not be possible to check the reliability of the findings.
- It may not be possible to ask participants for their informed consent, and participants may be deceived and may not be debriefed, all of which are breaches of the British Psychological Society (BPS) ethical guidelines.

Natural experiments
A natural experiment is one in which, rather than being manipulated by the researcher, the IV to be studied is naturally occurring. Some examples of naturally occurring variables are gender, age, ethnicity, occupation, smoker or non-smoker. When the IV is naturally occurring, participants cannot be randomly allocated between conditions. A natural experiment may take place in a laboratory or in a field experimental setting.

Strengths
- Natural experiments allow psychologists to study the effects of IVs that could be unethical to manipulate.
- When participants are unaware of the experiment, and the task is not contrived, research may have high internal validity.

Limitations
- Since participants cannot be allocated randomly between conditions, it is possible that random variables (individual differences other than the IV) can also affect the DV. This may lead to low internal validity.
- Natural experiments can be difficult to replicate with a different group of participants. It may not be possible to check the reliability of the findings.

Item 2   Correlational research

Correlation is a statistical technique used to calculate the correlation coefficient in order to quantify the strength of relationship between two variables. An example is whether there is a relationship between aggressive behaviour and playing violent video games.

Studies that use correlational analysis cannot draw conclusions about cause and effect. If a relationship is found between behaving aggressively and playing violent video games, individual differences in personality variables could be one factor that causes both of these. Just because two events (or behaviours) co-occur does not mean that one necessarily causes the other.

A correlation coefficient is a mathematical measure of the degree of relatedness between sets of data. Once calculated, it will have a value between –1 and +1:
- A **perfect positive correlation**, indicated by +1, is where as variable X increases, variable Y increases.
- A **perfect negative correlation**, indicated by –1, is where as variable X decreases, variable Y decreases.

Strengths
- Correlational analysis allows researchers to calculate the strength of a relationship between variables as a quantitative measure. A coefficient of +0.9 indicates a strong positive correlation; a coefficient of –0.3 may indicate a weak negative correlation.
- Where a correlation is found, it is possible to make predictions about one variable from the other.
- Correlation is useful as a pointer for more detailed research.

Limitations
- Researchers cannot assume that one variable causes the other.
- Correlation between variables may be misleading and can be misinterpreted.
- A lack of correlation may not mean there is no relationship, because the relationship could be non-linear. For example, there is a relationship between physiological arousal and performance, but the relationship is expressed by a curve, not by a straight line. The Yerkes-Dodson curve shows that a little arousal improves performance but too much reduces performance.

Analysing correlational data
- Data can be plotted as points on a scattergraph. A line of best fit is then drawn through the points to show the trend of the data (see Topic 3).
- If both variables increase together, this is a **positive correlation**.
- If one variable increases as the other decreases, this is a **negative correlation**.
- If no line of best fit can be drawn, there is **no correlation**.

Item 3   Interviews and questionnaire surveys

Psychologists often find out about people's behaviour by asking them about it. However, one of the main problems with this is that people like others to think well of them. As a result, what they say about their behaviour and how they actually behave may be different. There are several different ways in which psychologists conduct interviews and surveys.

Structured interviews
- All participants are asked the same questions in the same order.
- Structured interviews can be replicated and can be used to compare people's responses.
- They can be time consuming and require skilled researchers. People's responses can be affected by social desirability bias.

Unstructured interviews
- Participants can discuss anything freely and the interviewer devises new questions on the basis of answers previously given.
- They provide rich and detailed information but they are not replicable and people's responses cannot be compared.
- They can be time consuming and people's responses can be affected by social desirability bias. They also require trained interviewers.

Questionnaires
- Questionnaires are usually written, but can be conducted face to face, or completed over the telephone or on the internet.
- Printed questionnaires are completed by participants. They are similar to structured interviews in that all participants are asked the same questions in the same order. They usually restrict participants to a narrow range of answers.
- Questionnaires are a practical way to collect a large amount of information quickly and they can be replicated. Problems can arise if the questions are unclear or if they suggest a 'desirable' response, as responses can be affected by social desirability bias. When closed questions are used, participants cannot explain their answers.

Item 4   Naturalistic observations

When psychologists conduct a naturalistic observation, they watch people's behaviour but remain inconspicuous and do nothing to change or interfere with it.

Strengths
- Behaviour can be observed in its normal setting, and usually there are no problems with demand characteristics, unless the situation in which the participants are being observed has been specially contrived.
- It is useful when researching children or animals.
- It can be a useful way to gather data for a pilot study.

Limitations

- No explanation for the observed behaviour is gained because the observer counts instances of behaviour but does not ask participants to explain why they acted as they did.
- Observers may 'see what they expect to see' (observer bias) or may miss, or misinterpret, behaviour.
- Studies are difficult to replicate.

Item 5   The case study method

A case study is a detailed study into the life and background of one person (or of a small group of people). Case studies involve looking at past records, such as school and health records, and asking other people about the participant's past and present behaviour. Case studies are often done on people who have unusual abilities or difficulties. An example of a case study is Thigpen and Cleckley, 'The three faces of Eve'.

Strengths

- Case studies give a detailed picture of an individual and help to discover how a person's past may be related to his or her present behaviour.
- They can form a basis for future research.
- By studying the unusual, we can learn more about the usual.

Limitations

- Case studies may rely on memory, which may be inaccurate or distorted.
- They can only tell you about one person, so findings can never be generalised.
- The interviewer may be biased and/or the interviewee may not tell the truth.
- Retrospective studies may rely on memory, which may be biased or faulty or incomplete. Also, past records may be incomplete.

Item 6   Ethical research

Psychological research seeks to improve our understanding of human nature, and ethics are standards regarding what is right or wrong. An ethical issue occurs when there is conflict, for example between what the researcher wants in order to conduct valid or meaningful research and the rights of participants. The problematic question is whether psychological research is justifiable, usually in terms of how the participants are treated, but sometimes in terms of how the findings or conclusions may be applied.

Ethical guidelines

The British Psychological Society (BPS) has issued a set of ethical guidelines designed to protect the wellbeing and dignity of research participants. The following is adapted from 'Ethical principles for conducting research with human participants'. The complete text is available on the BPS website (www.bps.org.uk).

Good psychological research is possible only if there is mutual respect and confidence between investigators and participants. Ethical guidelines are necessary to clarify the conditions under which psychological research is acceptable.

In all circumstances, investigators must consider the ethical implications and psychological consequences for the participants in their research. It is essential that the investigation should be considered from the standpoint of all participants; and foreseeable threats to their psychological wellbeing, health, values or dignity should be eliminated.

Consent: whenever possible, the investigator should inform all participants of the objectives of the investigation. The investigator should inform the participants of all aspects of the research or intervention that might reasonably be expected to influence willingness to participate. Where research involves any persons under 16 years of age, consent should be obtained from parents or from those *in loco parentis*.

Deception: the misleading of participants is unacceptable if the participants are typically likely to object or show unease once debriefed. Where this is in any doubt, appropriate consultation must precede the investigation. Consultation is best carried out with individuals who share the social and cultural background of the participants. Intentional deception of the participants over the purpose and general nature of the investigation should be avoided whenever possible.

Debriefing: where the participants are aware that they have taken part in an investigation, when the data have been collected the investigator should provide the participants with any necessary information to complete their understanding of the nature of the research.

Withdrawal from the investigation: at the onset of the investigation, investigators should make plain to participants their right to withdraw from the research at any time, irrespective of whether or not payment or other inducement has been offered. The participant has the right to withdraw retrospectively any consent given, and to require that their own data, including recordings, be destroyed.

Confidentiality: subject to the requirements of legislation, including the Data Protection Act, information obtained about a participant during an investigation is confidential unless otherwise agreed in advance. Participants in psychological research have a right to expect that information they provide will be treated confidentially and, if published, will not be identifiable as theirs.

Protection of participants: investigators have a responsibility to protect participants from physical and mental harm during the investigation. Normally, the risk of harm must be no greater than in ordinary life, i.e. participants should not be exposed to risks greater than or additional to those encountered in their normal lifestyles. Where research may involve behaviour or experiences that participants may regard as personal and private, the participants must be protected from stress by all appropriate measures, including the assurance that answers to personal questions need not be given.

Observational research: studies based upon observation must respect the privacy and psychological wellbeing of the individuals studied. Unless those observed give their consent to being observed, observational research is only acceptable in situations where those observed would expect to be observed by strangers.

Giving advice: if, in the normal course of psychological research, a participant solicits advice concerning educational, personality, behavioural or health issues, caution should be exercised. If the issue is serious and the investigator is not qualified to offer assistance, the appropriate source of professional advice should be recommended.

Deception

It can be argued that if participants are not deceived about the true aims of a study, their behaviour may be affected and thus may not reflect how they would really behave in their everyday lives (i.e. participants show the effects of demand characteristics).

The dilemma for researchers is to design and conduct research that accurately portrays human behaviour while at the same time ensuring that they do not breach the ethical guidelines. Researchers may solve this dilemma by undertaking a cost–benefit analysis of the research before they commence a study. In other words, researchers should try to calculate the benefit of their research to psychology and to society, and try to assess the cost, in terms of potential harm, to their participants.

However, trying to balance potential benefits against potential costs raises problems:
- First, it is almost impossible to calculate the costs and benefits before a study, as the researchers cannot predict events accurately.
- Second, even after a study it is difficult to calculate the costs and benefits, as this may depend on when and who makes the judgement. The value of some research may not become apparent immediately and participants, and even other researchers, may judge the benefits and costs differently.
- Third, this approach may encourage researchers to ignore the rights of the individual participants on the grounds that 'many more people will benefit'.

Informed consent

All participants should be asked to give informed consent prior to taking part in research. However, in some situations where deception may be used, it is not possible to obtain fully informed consent from the participants of the study and psychologists propose the following alternatives:
- **Presumptive consent:** when presumptive consent is gained, people who are members of the population who are to be studied are informed of the details of the study and asked whether, if they were to participate, they would consider the research acceptable. Note that these 'potential participants' do not comprise the actual sample of participants.
- **Prior general consent:** this involves asking questions of people who have volunteered to participate, before they are selected to take part. For example:
  – Would you mind being involved in a study in which you were deceived?

– Would you mind taking part in a study if you were not informed of its true objectives?
– Would you mind taking part in a study that might cause you some stress?
Participants who say they would not mind may later be selected to participate, and it is
assumed they have agreed in principle to the conditions of the study.

- **Retrospective consent:** some psychologists argue that if participants are fully debriefed,
  and told if they were in any way deceived, and informed that they may withdraw their data,
  then this counts as retrospective consent. Giving participants the right to withdraw their data
  afterwards has the same effect as participants refusing to take part in the first place. Others
  would argue that if embarrassed participants choose to withdraw their data, this does not
  nullify the psychological effect on them of unethical research.

Research methods and ethical issues

Each research method raises different ethical issues:

- **Laboratory experiment:** even when told they have the right to withdraw, participants may
  feel reluctant to do so and may feel they should do things they would not normally do.
  Participants may be deceived.
- **Field experiment:** it may be difficult to obtain informed consent and participants may not be
  able to withdraw. It may be difficult to debrief the participants.
- **Natural experiment:** confidentiality may be a problem as the sample studied may be
  identifiable. Where naturally occurring social variables are studied (for example family income
  or ethnicity), ethical issues may arise when drawing conclusions and publishing the findings.
- **Correlational studies:** ethical issues can arise when researching relationships between
  socially sensitive variables (for example ethnicity and IQ) because published results can be
  misinterpreted as suggesting 'cause and effect'.
- **Interviews and questionnaires:** participants should not be asked embarrassing questions
  (protection from psychological harm) and should be reminded that they do not have to
  answer any questions if they do not wish to. Protecting confidentiality is important.
- **Naturalistic observations:** if informed consent is not being gained, people should only be
  observed in public places and where they would not be distressed to find they were being
  observed. If the location in which behaviour was observed is identifiable, an ethical issue
  may arise in terms of protecting confidentiality.

Questions

1 Read Items 1–6.

  a Describe *one* difference between a laboratory experiment and a field experiment.

  > A lab experiment is based in a controlled laboratory
  > environment where extraneous variables can be minimised.
  > Whereas a field experiment is set in a real life environment
  > such as a train station, where other variables can affect the DV

b Outline *one* advantage and *one* disadvantage of laboratory experiments.

⊕ High levels of control, so the DU can be sure to be being affected directly by the IV, no extraneous variables.
⊖ Low ecological validity, the environment is different to what (Ps) are used to, may present demand characteristics (DC's)

c Outline *one* advantage and *one* disadvantage of using the field experiment method.

⊕ High ecological validity and where (Ps) aren't aware of the experiment this method has no (DC's).
⊖ Low level of control, because of the environment the researchers cannot stop all extraneous variables.

d What is the defining characteristic of a natural experiment?

The Independent Variable is naturally occuring (such as gender, hair colour or eye colour) and is not manipulated for the purposes of the study).

e Explain *one* advantage of using the case study method.

⊕ Lots of in-depth information and detail about the participants, which is useful for the purpose of the experiment.

f Explain why the results of case studies cannot be generalised to anyone other than the participant(s).

Information gained from that person / group of people can only be used to describe those (Ps) as all of the study was conducted with them, so it can only be used for them.

2 A housing estate is being built next to Learnalot School. There are two classes of Year 6 children. The teachers are concerned that the Year 6 children whose classroom is on the side of the school next to the noisy building site will be distracted from their lessons and will learn less than the Year 6 children whose classroom is on the quiet side of the school. They decide to conduct some research to collect evidence as to the effect of the building-site noise. They design a test to be administered to the 'noisy' and 'quiet' side Year 6 children. The test comprises 100 questions and each correct answer scores 1 point. (The test is based on what the children have been taught over a 2-week period, and both classes have the same lessons.)

a Explain whether the research method the teachers decide to use is a laboratory experiment, a field experiment or a natural experiment.

Natural experiment - because the two groups have already been created, so there are already 2 conditions that are naturally occuring.

b Identify the IV and the DV in this experiment.

- IV is if the children are on the "Noisy / Quiet" condition
- DV is their score on the 100 question test.

c Are the data to be collected quantitative or qualitative?

The data will be quantitative, the (Ps) scores on a test.

d List three extraneous variables that would be difficult for the teachers to control.

- The students' learning ability for the two week period.
- Individual differences, such such as past experience
- Their ability to do well on tests.

e Outline what the teachers should do to ensure that they comply with the BPS ethical guidelines to protect the child participants in their research.

Get concent from the childrens parents to comply with concent with children. Also, the children should be informed that they have the right to withdraw at

any time and guaranteed anonymity from the studies
results etc.

3 Read Item 2.

 a Explain what a 'positive correlation' between two variables means.

  A positive correlation is where a relationship of mutual
  increase (as x increases, so does y) is occuring.

 b Which graphical technique should be used to display a correlation?

  Scatter-diagram.

 c Outline *one* advantage and *one* disadvantage of correlational methodology.

  ⊕ Allows for a relationship between two variables to be
  identified, so predictions could be made about further inferences.
  ⊖ However, a correlation cannot be used to imply
  Cause and effect as they could just be co-occuring.

4 A university lecturer wonders whether there is a relationship between student attendance
  at lectures and their achievement in exams. She finds a positive correlation between the
  number of lectures attended and scores in the exam. As the number of lectures increases so
  do exam scores. She is so impressed by the findings of her research that she puts a notice
  up outside the lecture hall telling students that if they do not attend her lectures they will
  fail their exams.

  Explain why this message may not be a valid conclusion to draw from her findings.

  Correlation does not mean causation, there could be
  a number of other variables causing the higher scores
  in exams. Also, the correlation could be non-linear, giving
  different results at opposing ends of the spectrum. (e.g.
  Yerkes-dodson curve).

5 Read your textbook and Items 3–6.

a When using the interview method, researchers may use structured or unstructured interview techniques. Explain how these differ.

b Outline *one* advantage of using self-report methods to collect information.

6 A psychologist wishes to investigate early child development, so she designs a questionnaire asking about infants' social behaviour and gives these to mothers of young children.

a Explain *one* disadvantage of using questionnaires to collect these data.

b Some of the questions collect quantitative data. Explain *one* advantage of collecting quantitative data.

c One of the questions collects qualitative data. Explain *one* advantage of collecting qualitative data.

d Explain how the psychologist could deal with ethical issues arising from this study.

7 Refer to Items 4 and 6.

A researcher wishes to undertake an observational study of aggression in toddlers.

a Suggest how types of aggression could be categorised for this observation.

b Outline *one* advantage and *one* disadvantage of research using naturalistic observations.

c Suggest *two* ethical issues that this researcher may encounter and how each of these issues might be dealt with.

....

....

....

....

....

....

....

....

Research methods
Topic 2 Investigation design

In this topic, you will learn how psychologists design research, formulate hypotheses, operationalise the research variables and select participants. You will also learn about techniques for assessing and improving validity and reliability.

Item 1 Aims and hypotheses

A **research aim** is a general statement of the purpose of the study but is not precise enough to test. It should make clear what the study intends to investigate.

A **hypothesis** states precisely what the researcher believes to be true about the target population. It is often generated from a theory and is a testable statement.

The term '**experimental hypothesis**' is used when experimental research is being conducted (laboratory, field or natural experiments); otherwise the term '**alternative hypothesis**' is used. The experimental hypothesis states that some difference (or effect) will occur: that the IV will have a significant effect on the DV. The **null hypothesis** is a statement of no difference or of no correlation — the IV does not affect the DV — and is what is tested by the inferential statistical test.

If data analysis forces researchers to reject the **null hypothesis**, because a significant effect is found, they then accept the experimental/alternative hypothesis. The experimental hypothesis can be directional or non-directional:
- **A directional hypothesis** is termed a 'one-tailed hypothesis' because it predicts the direction in which the results are expected to go. Directional hypotheses are used when previous research evidence suggests that it is possible to make a clear prediction about the way in which the IV will affect the DV.
- A **non-directional hypothesis** is termed a 'two-tailed hypothesis' because, although researchers expect the IV will affect the DV, they are not sure how.

Item 2 Research design

Independent groups design
Different participants are used in each of the conditions.
- **Advantages**: no participants are 'lost' between trials. Participants can be randomly allocated between the conditions to distribute individual differences evenly. There are no practice effects.
- **Disadvantages**: it needs more participants and there may be important differences between the groups to start with that are not removed by the random allocation of participants between conditions.

Repeated measures design

The same group of participants is used in each of the conditions.

- **Advantages:** it requires fewer participants. It controls for individual differences between participants as, in effect, the participants are compared against themselves.
- **Disadvantages:** it cannot be used in studies in which participation in one condition will affect responses in another (for example where participants learn tasks). It cannot be used in studies where an order effect would create a problem.

When a repeated measures design is used, problems may arise from participants doing the same task twice. The second time they carry out the task, they may be better than the first time because they have had practice, or worse than the first time because they have lost interest or are tired. If this happens, then an **order effect** is occurring.

One way that researchers control for order effects is to use a **counterbalancing technique**. The group of participants is split and half the group completes condition A followed by condition B; the other half completes condition B followed by condition A. In this way, any order effects are balanced out.

Matched pairs (matched participants) design

Separate groups of participants are used who are matched on a one-to-one basis on characteristics such as age or gender, to control for the possible effect of individual differences.

- **Advantages:** matching participants controls for some individual differences. It can be used when a repeated measures design is not appropriate, for example when performing the task twice would result in a practice effect.
- **Disadvantages:** a large number of prospective participants is often needed, from which to select matched pairs, and it is difficult to match on some characteristics (for example personality). More participants are needed than in a repeated measures design.

Item 3   Factors associated with research design

Operationalisation of variables: the term 'operationalisation' means being able to define variables in order to manipulate the IV and measure the DV. However, some variables are easier to operationalise than others. For example, performance on a memory test might be operationalised as 'the number of words remembered', but it is more difficult to operationalise how stressed someone may be. You could operationalise stress by measuring physiological arousal, or you could ask participants to rate how stressed they are. Both the IV and the DV need to be precisely operationalised, otherwise, the results may not be valid and cannot be replicated because another researcher would not be able to set up a study to repeat the same measurements.

Standardised instructions and procedures: all participants should be told what to do in exactly the same way, and all participants should be treated in exactly the same way.

Control of variables: any variables that change between the conditions, other than the IV, are difficult to control (for example how tired the participants are). Environmental variables that may affect participants' performance, such as the time of day or location, also need to be controlled.

Pilot studies: research is expensive in terms of both time and money, and no piece of research is perfect. To establish whether the design works, that participants can understand the instructions, that nothing has been missed out, and that participants are able to do what is asked, a pilot study (a trial run with a small number of participants) should be undertaken. This allows researchers to make necessary adjustments and to save wasting valuable resources.

Item 4   Reliability and validity

Reliability
Reliability of results means consistency. In other words, if something is measured more than once, the same effect should result. If my tape measure tells me I am 152 cm tall one day but 182 cm tall the next, then the tape measure I am using is not reliable.

Internal reliability refers to how consistently a method measures within itself, for example my tape measure should measure the same distance between 0 cm and 10 cm as it does between 10 cm and 20 cm. To test for internal reliability, researchers may use the **split-half technique**, in which half of the scores are compared with the other half to see how similar they are.

External reliability refers to the consistency of measures over time (i.e. if repeated). For example, personality tests should not give different results if the same person is tested more than once. External reliability can be tested by the **test–retest method**. For example, the same participants can be tested on more than one occasion to see whether their results remain similar.

Inter-observer reliability assesses whether, in an observational study, if several observers are coding behaviour, their codings or ratings agree with each other. To improve reliability, all observers must have clear and operationalised categories of behaviour and must be trained how to use the system. Inter-observer reliability can be measured using correlational analysis, in which a high positive correlation among ratings indicates that high inter-observer reliability has been established.

Validity

Internal validity
This refers to the extent to which a measurement technique measures what it is supposed to, whether the IV really caused the effect on the DV or whether some other factor was responsible. Experiments may lack internal validity because of demand characteristics, participant reactivity, or because extraneous variables have not been controlled.

Another aspect of internal validity is **mundane realism**, i.e. do the measures used generalise to real life? For example, does a measure of long-term memory based on remembering lists of words generalise to how people really remember past events? Mundane realism is an aspect of internal validity that contributes to external validity.

External (ecological) validity

This refers to the validity of a study outside the research situation and provides some idea of the extent to which the findings can be generalised. To assess the external validity of research, three questions should be considered:

- How representative is the sample of participants of the population to which the results are to be generalised? (**population validity**)
- Do the research setting and situation generalise to a realistic real-life setting or situation? (**ecological validity**)
- Do the findings generalise to the past and to the future? (**ecological or historical validity**) For example, it is argued that 50 years ago people were more conformist and obedient.

Item 5 Research participants

Selecting participants

When researchers conduct research, the **target population** is the group of people to whom they wish to generalise their findings. The **sample** of participants is the group of people that takes part in the study, and a **representative sample** is a sample of people who are representative of the target population. There are several ways in which researchers select a sample.

Random sampling

This involves having the names of the target population and giving everyone an equal chance of being selected. A random sample can be selected by a computer or, in a small population, by selecting names from a hat.

- **Advantage:** a true random sample avoids bias, as every member of the target population has an equal chance of being selected.
- **Disadvantage:** it is almost impossible to obtain a truly random sample because not all the names of the target population may be known.

Opportunity sampling

This involves asking whoever is available and willing to participate. An opportunity sample is not likely to be representative of any target population because it will probably comprise friends of the researcher, or students, or people in a specific workplace. The people approached will be those who are local and available, and they are likely to comprise a biased sample of participants who are not representative of any wider population. A sample of participants approached 'in the street' is *not* a random sample of the population of a town. To be a random sample, all the people living in a town would have an equal opportunity to participate. In an opportunity sample, only the people present at the time the researcher was

seeking participants would be able to participate.
- **Advantage:** the researchers can quickly and inexpensively acquire a sample, and face-to-face ethical briefings and debriefings can be undertaken.
- **Disadvantage:** opportunity samples are almost always biased samples, as who participates is dependent on who is asked and who happens to be available at the time.

Volunteer sampling

Volunteer samples mean exactly that: people who volunteer to participate. A volunteer sample may not be representative of the target population because there may be differences between the sort of people who volunteer and those who do not.
- **Advantage:** the participants should have given their informed consent, will be interested in the research and may be less likely to withdraw.
- **Disadvantage:** a volunteer sample may be a biased sample that is not representative of the target population because volunteers may be different in some way to non-volunteers. For example, they may be more helpful (or more curious) than non-volunteers.

Sample representativeness

Researchers wish to apply the findings of their research in order to learn and explain something about the behaviour of the target population, thus the sample of participants should be a true representation of diversity in the target population. In psychological research, students are often used as participants, but an all-student sample is only representative of a target population of students. Likewise, an all-male sample may only be representative of an all-male target population. If the sample is not representative, then the research findings cannot be generalised to the target population.

Researchers also need to decide how many participants are needed, and the number required depends on several factors:
- The sample must be large enough to be representative of the target population.
- If the target population is small, then it may be possible, and sensible, to use the whole population as the sample. However, there is unlikely to be that small a target population in a psychology study.
- The sample needs to be a manageable size, as too many participants make research expensive and time consuming.
- If the research has important implications, for example testing a new drug, the sample size should be larger than it would be in a less important study.
- In small samples, the individual differences between participants will have a greater effect. If the effect being studied is likely to be small, then a larger sample will be required.

Item 6   The relationship between researchers and participants

In any research project, the interaction between researchers and participants needs to be considered. Problems can arise because of the behaviour of the researcher or of the participants.

Participant effects

When people know they are being studied, their behaviour is affected. Regardless of other variables, as soon as people know their behaviour is of interest, it is likely to change. Some ways in which participation in research can affect behaviour are as follows:

- **The Hawthorne effect:** if people are aware that they are being studied, they are likely to try harder on tasks and pay more attention. This may mean that any findings (for example response times) are artificially high, which may lead to invalid conclusions.
- **Demand characteristics:** sometimes, features of the research situation, the research task, and possibly the researcher, may give cues to participants as to what is expected of them or how they are expected to behave, or in some way change participant behaviour. This may lead to response bias, in which participants try to please the experimenter (or deliberately do the opposite), in which case conclusions drawn from the findings may be invalid. Demand characteristics may be reduced if a **single-blind procedure** is used. Here, participants do not know which condition they are participating in, or are given a false account of the experiment. If a single-blind procedure is used, ethical issues arise because fully informed consent cannot be gained. However, if features of the research task cue participants to change their behaviour, a single-blind procedure will not control for this.
- **Social desirability bias:** people usually try to show themselves in the best possible way. So when answering questions in interviews or questionnaires, they may give answers that are socially acceptable but that are not truthful. For example, people tend to under-report antisocial behaviour, such as alcohol consumption and smoking, and over-report prosocial behaviour, such as giving to charity. If questions asked as part of a research project have answers that might be perceived as more or less socially desirable, it is important to be aware that answers might not be truthful and that the conclusions drawn from the findings may be invalid.

Investigator and/or experimenter effects

An investigator is the person who designs the study, and an experimenter is the person who conducts the study; this may or may not be the same person. Researchers may unwittingly affect the results of their research in several ways:

- **Investigator expectancy:** the expectations of the researcher can affect how he or she designs the research and bias how and what he or she decides to measure, and how the findings are analysed.
- **Experimenter bias:** the experimenter can affect the way participants behave. One way to reduce experimenter effects is to use a **double-blind procedure**, in which neither the experimenter nor the participants know what the research hypothesis is.
- **Interviewer effects:** the expectations of the interviewer may lead him or her to ask only those questions in which he or she is interested, or to ask leading questions, or he or she may only focus on answers that match his or her expectations.
- **Observer bias:** when observing behaviour, observers may make biased interpretations of the meaning of behaviour.

Questions

1 Review the items in Topics 1 and 2.

Some research suggests that ageing may have a negative effect on memory. Imagine you are going to design a research project to find out whether students have better memories than teachers.

a State your research aim.

....

....

b State the method you will use in your research and explain why you chose this method.

....

....

....

....

c Write a testable one-tailed experimental hypothesis for your study.

....

....

....

d Write a testable two-tailed experimental hypothesis for your study.

....

....

....

e Write a null hypothesis for your study.

....

....

....

f Identify the IV in your study and describe how you will operationalise it.

....

....

....

g Identify the DV in your study and describe how you will operationalise it.

....

....

....

....

2 Read Items 2–4.

a Identify *two* research designs you could use in the study you designed in Question 1.

....

....

....

....

b Explain which research design you will use and why you made this decision, in terms of the advantages and disadvantages of the design.

....

....

....

....

....

....

c Identify *one* personal or environmental variable that you think will be important to control in the study you designed.

....

....

....

....

d Explain why you think controlling this factor will be important.

....

....

3 Read your textbook and Items 5 and 6, and then complete sentences **a–h**.

a A sample is only a random sample when…

b A sample is an opportunity sample when…

c A representative sample means that…

d A sample is said to be biased when the participants…

e A large sample is needed when…

f In a small sample, the findings may be invalid because…

g If a researcher stops people and asks them to participate in research, the resulting sample is called an _____ because…

h A matched sample increases the validity of the findings because…

....

....

....

4 Read your textbook and Items 5 and 6. Write definitions for the following:

a a random sample

....

....

b a volunteer sample

....

....

c an opportunity sample

....

....

5 In a college survey investigating student drinking habits, outline why social desirability bias may affect the student responses to questions about their alcohol consumption and explain how this could affect the findings.

....

....

....

....

....

6 Read your textbook and Items 5 and 6. In Question 1 you were asked to imagine you were designing a research project to find out whether students have better memories than teachers.

a Describe the population you are going to study.

....

....

b Describe how you will select a sample from this population.

....

....

....

....

c Identify *one* potential ethical issue that your investigation might raise and describe the precautions you would take to deal with this issue.

....

....

....

....

....

7 *Exam-style question*

Many people complain that they become more forgetful when they get older. Some people say that they never forget a face but they do not remember names; a few people are memory prodigies who can remember whole telephone directories; and some people suggest that women have better memories than men.

These interesting facts raise psychological research questions, such as:
- Is memory less effective in older people?
- Are pictures easier to remember than words?
- Do females have better memories than males?

Imagine *you* are going to design a research project to answer *one* of these questions.

a State your research aim.

....

....

....

b State the method you will use in your research and explain why you chose this method.

....

....

....

c Write a testable one-tailed experimental hypothesis for your study and explain why this hypothesis is one-tailed.

....

....

....

....

....

d Write a testable two-tailed experimental hypothesis for your study and explain why this hypothesis is two-tailed.

....

....

....

....

....

e Write a null hypothesis for your study.

....

....

....

f Identify the IV in your study and describe how you will operationalise it.

....

....

....

....

g Identify the DV in your study and describe how you will operationalise it.

....

....

....

....

h Explain which research design you will use and why, in terms of the advantages and disadvantages of the design, you made this decision.

....

....

....

....

....

....

i Identify *one* personal or environmental variable that you think will be important to control in the study you designed.

....

....

....

....

j Explain why you think controlling this factor will be important.

....

....

....

....

....

....

Research methods
Topic 3 Data analysis and presentation of data

In this topic, you will learn how to:
- present data in research reports
- analyse data using descriptive statistics and the calculation of measures of central tendency and dispersion

You also need to be able to interpret correlational data and select the appropriate way to present data using charts and graphs.

Item 1 Data derived from observations, interviews and questionnaires

Observations, interviews and questionnaires can result in qualitative and/or quantitative data. In interviews and observations, qualitative data might result from video or audio recordings or written notes. Likewise, qualitative data can result when open questions are asked in interviews or questionnaires, or when participants are invited to explain why they behave in a certain way. It is important when analysing qualitative data that researchers avoid subjective or biased misinterpretations. Misinterpretation can be avoided by:
- using accurate language to operationalise the variables to be measured; for example, if observing play-fighting in children, an operationalised definition might be 'hitting while smiling' (though counting the frequency of this would be quantitative data)
- using a team of observers who have verified that they have achieved inter-observer reliability
- converting qualitative data into quantitative data; one way to do this is by coding the data

Coding qualitative data
- A sample of qualitative data is collected, for example from the interviewee, from magazines or newspapers, or from the notes or recordings of an observation.
- Coding units are identified in order to categorise the data. A coding unit could be specific words or phrases that are looked for (the operationalised definitions).
- The coding units may then be counted to see how frequently they occur. The resulting frequency of occurrence is a form of quantitative data.

Qualitative data
- **Advantages:** rich and detailed, collected in real-life settings, can be used to collect data on attitudes, opinions and beliefs.
- **Disadvantages:** may be subjective, can be an imprecise measure, may be low in reliability.

Quantitative data
- **Advantages:** objective, precise measures used, data are high in reliability and it is possible to see patterns in the data.
- **Disadvantages:** may lack or lose detail, often collected in contrived settings.

Item 2 Descriptive statistics

Descriptive statistics describe research findings. Measures of central tendency and dispersion are used to summarise large amounts of data into typical or average values, and to provide information on the variability or spread of the scores.

Measures of central tendency
There are three ways to calculate the average of a set of scores: the mean, the median and the mode.

Mean
All the scores are added up and the total is divided by the number of the scores. For example, take the following set of scores:

1	2	2	3	3	4	5	5	7	8

The mean of this set of scores is 4 (40 divided by10).
- **Advantages:** the mean is a sensitive measure — it takes all the values from the raw scores into account.
- **Disadvantages:** the mean can give a distorted impression if there are unusual scores (extremely high or low) in the data set. Often, the mean may have a 'meaningless' decimal point that was not in the original scores, for example 2.4 children.

Median
The median is the central score in a list of rank-ordered scores. In an odd number of scores, the median is the middle number. In an even numbered set of scores, the median is the mid-point between the two middle scores. For example, take the following set of scores:

2	3	4	5	5	6	7	8	15	16

The median of this set of scores is 5 + 6 divided by 2 = 5.5.
The mean of this set of scores is 7.1 (71 divided by10).
- **Advantages:** the median is not affected by extreme scores. It is useful when scores are ordered data (1st, 2nd, 3rd etc.).
- **Disadvantages:** the median does not take account of the values of all of the scores and can be misleading if used in small sets of scores.

Mode

The mode is the score that occurs most frequently in a set of scores. For example, take the following set of scores:

| 4 | 4 | 4 | 4 | 5 | 6 | 10 | 12 | 12 | 14 |

The mode of this set of scores is 4, because it occurs four times (the most frequently).

The median of this set of scores is 5 + 6 divided by 2 = 5.5.

The mean of this set of scores is 7.5 (75 divided by 10). This example shows that each of the measures of central tendency may describe the mid-point of a set of scores differently.

- **Advantages:** the mode is not affected by extreme scores. It may make more sense — avoiding nonsensical measures such as '2.4 children'.
- **Disadvantages:** the mode tells us nothing about other scores. There may be more than one mode in a set of data.

Measures of dispersion

Measures of dispersion tell us about the range of the scores, i.e. how far spread out they are.

- **Advantage:** they are easy and quick to work out and include extreme values.
- **Disadvantage:** they may be misleading when there are extremely high or low scores in a set.

Standard deviation

Standard deviation is used to measure how the scores are distributed around the central point (the mean). The greater the standard deviation, the larger the spread of the scores. If the scores are 'normally distributed', we would expect 66% of the scores in each set to lie within one standard deviation above or below the mean for the set.

- **Advantages:** standard deviation allows for an interpretation of any individual score in a set, and is particularly useful in large sets of scores. It is a sensitive measure of dispersion because all the scores are used in its calculation.
- **Disadvantages:** standard deviation is not useful when data are not normally distributed and is quite complicated to calculate.

Item 3   Graphs and charts

Psychologists use graphs and charts to summarise their data in visual displays. Information displayed in this way makes it easier for others to understand the findings of research.

Scattergraphs

Scattergraphs (scattergrams) are used to depict the results of correlational analysis. You can see at a glance whether there appears to be a positive, negative or no correlation.

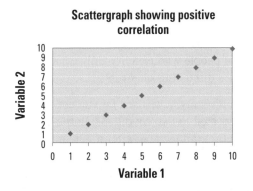

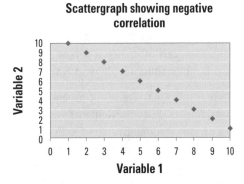

Bar charts

Bar charts are used when scores are in categories, when there is no fixed order for the items on the *y*-axis, or can be used to show a comparison of means for continuous data. The bar chart below shows the holiday destinations chosen by a sample of 300 families. The bars in bar charts should be the same width but do not touch. The space between the bars illustrates that the variable on the *x*-axis is discrete data.

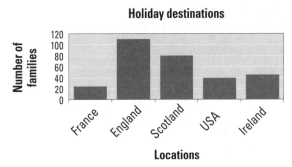

Histograms

Histograms use columns to show frequency distributions of continuous data, and there should be no gaps between the bars.

This example shows the exam results (marks) for a class of 30 students in a mock exam marked out of a maximum of 100. The scores have been grouped into ranges of 10 marks.

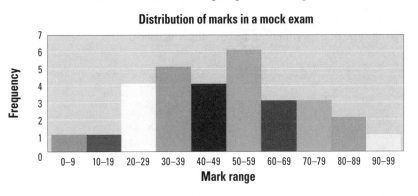

Questions

1 Can watching television make people feel happier? Research has suggested that watching television can influence a person's mood, and that people who watch mainly comedy shows feel happier than people who watch documentaries discussing sad events.

To test this idea, a team of psychologists from a university advertised for student participants. Fifty participants were randomly allocated to two conditions. In the 'sad last' condition, students watched a 35-minute comedy programme and, after a 2-hour break, they watched a 35-minute documentary in which survivors talked about the death and destruction caused by an earthquake. In the 'comedy last' condition, students watched the same 35-minute documentary about the earthquake and, after the same length break, they watched the 35-minute comedy programme. After they had watched both programmes, a questionnaire was used to measure the participants' mood. Scores ranged from 10 to 40, where high scores indicated feeling happy.

Condition	Mean	Standard deviation
Sad last	20.80	3.60
Comedy last	26.44	5.37

a State the aim of the research described above.

b Describe the operationalised independent variable and the operationalised dependent variable for this experiment.

c Identify the type of experimental design that was used.

d Give *one* advantage and *one* disadvantage of this design.

....

....

....

....

....

....

....

e Explain why the experiment was designed in such a way that half the participants saw the comedy programme first and the other half of the participants saw the sad programme first.

....

....

....

....

....

f Give *one* advantage of using the mean.

....

....

....

g What does standard deviation tell us about data?

....

....

....

h Provide a suitably labelled visual diagram to depict the findings of this research.

i Give *one* conclusion that can be drawn from your visual diagram. *Hint*: Write the conclusion in terms of the research aim.

j This study used the experimental method. Briefly describe how you would use a method other than an experimental method to investigate the same aims.

2 A local authority in a university town has received complaints about drunken antisocial behaviour by students. To find out the frequency of binge drinking in the student population, the local authority asked a group of psychologists to design a questionnaire to be used in a survey of local students. An extract from the questionnaire is set out below.

1 Do you drink alcoholic drinks?   **Yes/No**
2 How many units of alcohol do you consume, on average, each week? _____
3 Would you describe yourself as a binge drinker?   **Yes/No**
4 How would you describe a binge drinker?

....

....

....

5 Have you ever behaved in an antisocial manner while drunk?   **Yes/No**
6 Do you ever regret drinking so much alcohol? Underline the option that applies to you.
   very often   often   rarely   never
7 Why do you consume alcoholic drinks?

a Outline *one* advantage and *one* disadvantage of using a questionnaire for the research
   described above.

....

....

....

....

....

b Explain *one* reason why a pilot study should have been carried out in the context of this
   survey.

....

....

....

....

....

....

c Identify *one* question in the questionnaire that would provide qualitative data. Explain why this question would produce qualitative data.

....

....

....

....

....

....

d Identify *one* sampling method that could have been used in this survey, and give one reason for choosing this method.

....

....

....

....

....

....

....

....

e Select *one* question from the questionnaire and give *one* criticism of it.

....

....

....

....

f Rewrite the question you selected in e so that it overcomes the criticism you identified.

....

....

....

....

....

g Describe *two* ways of making sure that this survey would be carried out in an ethically acceptable way.

....

....

....

....

....

....

....

....

Research methods
Topic 4 Levels of data and inferential statistics

In this topic, you will learn how to identify different types of research data (levels of data) and how to decide which inferential (non-parametric) statistical test you should use to calculate the significance of research findings. You will also learn in brief about levels of significance and how the level of significance chosen is related to the possibility of making a type-1 or type-2 error.

Item 1   Levels of data

Nominal level data
These data concern frequencies of occurrence, for example:
- how many cars are red, green or blue
- how many people are left- or right-handed

The **mode** should be used as the measure of central tendency. It makes no sense to calculate the mean, because you cannot have 2.4 children or the average of 5 red cars and 2 blue cars.

Ordinal level data
These data can be ranked in order 1st, 2nd, 3rd etc.
The **median** (middle score) should be used as the measure of central tendency, because the mean can be affected by 'extreme' scores.

Interval level data
These data are measured on a fixed scale, for example height in inches or weight in grams. The **mean** (mathematical midpoint) should be used, because this gives a precise measure of the central tendency — but remember that the mean can be affected by 'extreme' scores.

Item 2   Significance

How do you know if your results are meaningful? Do they show that the IV affected the DV? How large an effect is needed to be considered significant?

If, for example, you give 25 people a memory test with 20 pictures, and another 25 people a memory test using 20 words, and the average number of pictures remembered is 15, but the average number of words remembered is 12, a test of significance will indicate the probability that the results occurred *because of* the IV (the difference between the conditions) as opposed to being the result of chance or uncontrolled factors.

Tests of statistical significance
When researchers collect two samples of data from, say, an experimental group (A) and a control group (B), the question they wish to answer is: 'Are the results for group A *significantly different* from those of group B?' To find their answer, they perform a **statistical test of**

difference. Such tests are called **inferential statistics** because the calculations are based on the mathematics of probability, which enables us to make inferences about a population from the samples we have looked at.

The inferential test provides us with a numerical value, and when we look at a **table of significance**, we can find the probability (p) that our findings reflect the underlying population.

Critical values

The table of significance lists critical values for different levels of significance, such as p = <0.01 or p = <0.05. Usually the probabilities are given along the top of the table, the sample size is shown in the left-hand column and critical values are shown in the body of the table.

A probability of p = < 0.01 means that the probability is less than 1 in 100 (1%) that the results could have occurred *if the null hypothesis is true*. Therefore we reject the null hypothesis and accept the alternative (experimental) hypothesis.

Levels of significance

Level	Probability	Significance	When used
1% level	($p < 0.01$)	Highly significant	Where we would want to take few chances
5% level	($p < 0.05$)	Significant	Acceptable level for psychology research
10% level	($p < 0.10$)	Marginal	May indicate need for better methodology

Item 3　Inferential statistics

(Your teacher will help you with this)

For the exam, you need to know when to use each non-parametric inferential statistical test, and to be able to explain why you selected the test. You will have to learn these, but you do not have to calculate the inferential statistic in the exam.

- The **Mann–Whitney U test** is a test of the significance of the difference between two conditions when an independent design has been used *and* the level of data collected is 'at least' ordinal.
- The **Wilcoxon matched pairs signed ranks test** is a test of the significance of the difference between two conditions when a repeated measures design has been used *and* the level of data collected is 'at least' ordinal.
- The **Chi-square test** of significance of association is used when nominal level data have been collected.
- The **Spearman's rho test** is appropriate when data are 'at least' ordinal and a correlational design is used. This inferential test calculates the correlation coefficient to find the probability that the relationship between variables is stronger than would occur by chance.

You may be asked to explain your choice of statistical test. If you selected a Mann–Whitney U test, an appropriate explanation would be: 'I wanted to find out whether the difference between the two experimental groups is significant and for an independent design with ordinal level data the Mann–Whitney U test is appropriate.'

Item 4   Type-1 and type-2 errors

When psychologists decide whether to reject or retain the null hypothesis, they look at the results of the statistical test. However, there is always the possibility that they may make an error:

- A **type-1 error** is deciding to reject the null hypothesis (in an experiment concluding that the IV did have a significant effect on the DV) when actually the result was due to chance or some other factor.
- A **type-2 error** is deciding to retain the null hypothesis (in an experiment concluding that the IV had no significant effect on the DV) when actually the result was caused by the IV.

The level of significance selected affects whether researchers are likely to make a type-1 error or a type-2 error. If researchers set the level of significance low at $p = <0.10$, they are more likely to make a type-1 error. However, if researchers set the level of significance high, for example at $p = <0.001$, they are more likely to make a type-2 error.

Questions

1 Read Item 1.

a A psychologist gave two groups of students a list of words to remember. He wanted to find out whether boys had better memories than girls.

Identify the level of data being collected and explain how you came to this decision.

....

....

....

....

b A psychologist carried out an observational study to find out whether male drivers were more likely to use their mobile phones than female drivers.

Identify the level of data being collected and explain how you came to this decision.

....

....

....

....

c A psychologist devised an IQ test. The maximum score was 100. What level of data are the scores?

....

....

....

....

d You take someone's temperature. Identify the level of data being collected and explain how you came to this decision.

....

....

....

2 Read Item 2.

a Explain what 'significant at a probability of $p = <0.01$' means.

....

....

....

....

b A psychologist carried out a study to find out whether boys engage in more rough-and-tumble play than girls. The null hypothesis was that there would be no difference in the amount of rough-and-tumble play behaviours in boys and girls. The findings were that boys did engage in more rough-and-tumble play behaviour. The difference was significant at a level of probability of $p = <0.01$.

Explain whether the psychologist should retain the null hypothesis or not.

....

....

....

....

....

c A psychologist carried out a study to find out whether age affects memory. Two groups of participants, one group aged 18 and one group aged 50, were given 5 minutes to learn a list of 20 words. The null hypothesis was that there would be no difference in the number of words remembered by the young and older participants. The findings were that, on average, the older participants remembered more words. The difference was significant at a level of probability of $p = <0.10$.

Explain whether the psychologist should retain the null hypothesis or not.

....

....

....

....

....

....

3 Read Item 3.

a Using the scenario in Question 2c above, identify the inferential statistical test that should be used to analyse the significance of the findings and explain why this test is appropriate.

....

....

....

....

b A psychologist carried out a study to find out whether brief physical exercise has a positive effect on mood. To do this, she asked participants to self-report their mood, on a scale of 0 = anxious to 10 = relaxed, before and after they skipped for 3 minutes. The experimental hypothesis was that participants would report being significantly more relaxed after brief physical exercise.

Identify the inferential statistical test that should be used to analyse the significance of the findings and explain why this test is appropriate.

....

....

....

....

....

c A psychologist wanted to find out whether there is a relationship between IQ scores and how students perform in an end-of-term test. She wrote a hypothesis that predicted there would be a positive correlation between these two variables.

Identify the inferential statistical test that should be used to analyse the significance of the findings and explain why this test is appropriate.

....

....

....

....

....

d A psychologist wanted to find out whether the children of parents who smoke are more likely to begin to smoke as teenagers. She devised a questionnaire asking teenagers the following questions:
- Do you smoke cigarettes?   Yes/No
- Do either of your parents smoke cigarettes?   Yes/No

(i)   Are these closed or open questions?

....

(ii) Do these questions collect quantitative or qualitative data?

....

(iii) What level of data is being collected?

....

....

(iv) The findings for this study were that the teenagers who reported that one of their parents smoked were more likely to report that they smoked. The association was significant at a level of probability of $p = <0.01$. Identify the inferential statistical test that should be used to analyse the significance of the findings and explain why this test is appropriate.

....

....

....

....

....

4 Read Items 1–4. A psychologist wanted to find out whether the temperature of the classroom affects student performance in exams. To do this, she devised a maths test in which the maximum score was 100. She divided a class of 17-year-olds into two groups. One group completed the test in a warm room and the other group completed the test in a cold room.

a Which level of data is being collected?

b Which is the appropriate statistical test that should be used to analyse the findings?

c Which level of significance do you think should be used to analyse the significance of the findings and why?

d If the psychologist sets the level of significance at $p = <0.001$, is she more likely to make a type-1 or a type-2 error? Explain your answer.

e Make *two* suggestions as to which variables, other than the temperature of the room, might affect the results.

f Explain how the researcher could control *one* of the variables you have identified.

....

....

....

....

....

5 *Exam-style question*

Many people believe that older people are more likely to forget things than younger people, and some people say that playing word games can improve their memory. Some research suggests that we remember pictures better than we remember words, and many people suggest that men are better at navigation skills than women.

This raises many research questions.
- Do older people forget more than younger people?
- Do people who play Scrabble have better memories than people who do not play Scrabble?
- Do people remember pictures better than they remember words?
- Are men better at map reading than women?

You are required to design a practical project to investigate *one* of the above questions. Your project must be an independent design and you must plan to collect at least ordinal level data. Your project must be one you could carry out.

Describe the procedure for your investigation, making it clear how you would measure the dependent variable and giving examples of the materials you would use.

Marks are awarded for the quality of your design, the detail you give, the replicability of your design and the appropriateness of your design for the research purpose. For replicability, your description should include:
- the type of sample and the way it was selected
- the allocation to groups
- a description of the test or questionnaire with examples of materials or questions
- the conditions and timings of the test, questionnaire or observation
- the scoring of the test, questionnaire or observation

a State the research question you will investigate.

....

....

....

b Write an operationalised hypothesis for your investigation.

....

....

....

....

c Which method and design will you use?

....

....

d Name the IV and the DV.

....

....

....

....

e Name the sampling method you will use and describe your sample.

....

....

....

....

f Describe the materials you will use.

....

....

....

....

....

....

g Describe the procedure. (Do not forget to say how you will allocate participants to the research conditions.)

....

....

....

....

....

....

....

....

....

....

....

....

h Describe any controls you plan to use.

....

....

....

....

i Explain how the scores are obtained.

....

....

....

....

....

j Briefly describe how you will analyse your data and say which statistical test you will use and explain why.

....

....

....

....

....

....

....

k If the results of your statistical test find that your experimental hypothesis is significant at $p = {<}0.05$, what does that mean?

....

....

....

l Describe *one* weakness of using an independent samples design for this research. Suggest how you could reduce the effects of this weakness.

....

....

....

....

....

....

m Outline *one* way in which you would take ethical issues into account in the conduct of this research.

....

....

....

....

....

n Discuss the ecological validity of the way you measured your dependent variable.

....

....

....

....

....

o Suggest *one* other aspect of your research question that you might investigate at a future date. Explain your answer.

....

....

....

....

....

In Unit G544, you are expected to have knowledge and understanding of, and to be able to evaluate, all approaches, perspectives, issues and debates introduced in the AS course, as well as the new issues and debates introduced for A2:

- The approaches are physiological, cognitive, individual differences, developmental and social.
- The perspectives are behaviourist and psychodynamic.
- The debates are free will vs determinism, nature vs nurture, reductionism vs holism, ethnocentrism, psychology as a science, individual vs situational explanations, and the usefulness of psychological research. Because you will have studied individual vs situational explanations for behaviour, and the question of the usefulness of psychological research at AS, these two debates are not included in this workbook. However, when you learn a new 'study', you should always be able to explain whether and how the study is useful in terms of its research aim.
- The issues, which you learned at AS and/or in the 'Research methods' section of this workbook, are ethics in psychological research, ecological validity, longitudinal vs snapshot studies, and qualitative vs quantitative data.

In the exam, synoptic questions on approaches, debates and issues will be in the form of structured questions. The aim of this section is to help you increase your understanding and to improve your skills in answering the types of question that you might encounter.

Item 1   The physiological approach

The physiological (biological) approach assumes that much of our behaviour can be explained in terms of our biological systems. A physiological explanation is one that refers to bodily activity.

For example, there are physiological theories about dreaming that are based solely on brain activity. It is claimed, using the physiological approach, that dreams are simply the random electrical activity of the brain during sleep upon which the mind imposes some sense.

A further example of a physiological account could be of stress, which would focus on how heart rate and breathing increase in the presence of a stressor.

However, it is doubtful whether we can explain all behaviour in terms of biological factors such as brain structure, genes or hormones. The physiological approach is thus said to be reductionist, because it reduces the complex nature of human activity to simple systems and ignores social, cognitive and other factors that have been shown to affect behaviour.

Assumptions of the physiological approach

- All behaviour can be explained and understood at the level of the functioning of physiological systems.
- There is a direct relationship between the physiology of the brain and body and human behaviour.
- Behaviour and experience can be reduced to the functioning of physiological systems.

Evaluation of the physiological approach

Strengths

- The objective, reductionist nature of physiological explanations facilitates experimental research.
- Physiological explanations can be used to treat dysfunctional behaviour, for example drug therapies are widely used to treat mental illnesses, often with a reasonable amount of success.
- Physiological explanations are scientific because they do not need us to infer metaphysical constructs such as 'mind' to explain human behaviour.

Weaknesses

- The physiological approach offers an objective, reductionist and mechanistic (machine-like) explanation of behaviour, which is over-simplistic.
- The physiological approach overlooks the experiential aspect of behaviour. It ignores past experience in our environment as an influence on behaviour.
- Physiological explanations are more appropriate for some kinds of behaviour (such as the physiology of stress), but whether a person feels stressed involves social and psychological factors, so physiological explanations alone are usually inadequate.
- Physiological explanations are deterministic, suggesting that all behaviour is entirely predictable.

Item 2   The cognitive approach

The cognitive approach assumes that internal, mental processes, such as those involved in perception, attention, language, memory and thinking, explain behaviour.

Cognitive psychology focuses on the way that mental or cognitive processes work and looks at how we input, store and retrieve information. Any research that looks at aspects of cognition, such as Griffith's cognitive bias in fruit-machine gambling and Loftus's research into aspects of memory, is using the cognitive approach.

Assumptions of the cognitive approach

- Behaviour can largely be explained in terms of how the mind operates.
- The mind works like a computer, inputting, storing and retrieving data.
- People make decisions as to how they behave.

Evaluation of the cognitive approach

Strengths

- The approach has useful applications, ranging from advice about the validity of eyewitness testimony and how to improve performance in situations requiring close attention (such as air traffic control) to successful therapies for psychological problems such as stress.

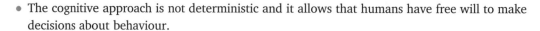

- The cognitive approach is not deterministic and it allows that humans have free will to make decisions about behaviour.

Weaknesses
- The cognitive approach tends to ignore social, motivational and emotional factors and assumes that humans are rational. It underemphasises the role of human emotion.
- Much research by cognitive psychologists is experimental and based in laboratories, in situations that lack ecological validity. For example, many memory experiments measure 'memory for facts', but there are many different kinds of memory.
- Mental processes are essentially private and can be difficult to reveal in non-experimental research.

Item 3   The individual differences approach

Psychologists need to take account of individual and cultural differences in their theories, and traditionally many research findings were based on white, middle-class American males, often students. This means that many of the traditional theories in psychology are explanations of the behaviour of a biased sample of human beings.

There are many areas of interest and debate within psychology, not least of which is the most fundamental question of 'what is normal?', especially when considering explanations for dysfunctional behaviour.

In some instances, there are biological causes for dysfunctional behaviour. For example, Down's syndrome is caused by an extra chromosome, but some Down's individuals are severely affected whereas others have quite a mild form of the condition. Rosenhan's classic study raises issues about the validity and reliability of the diagnosis of normality/abnormality, especially when the dysfunction has no identifiable physical cause. The individual differences approach treats each person as unique and often uses case study methodology.

A case study is a detailed study into the life and background of one person (or of a small group of people). Case studies involve looking at past records, such as school and health records, and asking other people about the participant's past and present behaviour. Case studies are often undertaken to explain the causes of unusual abilities or behaviour, for example Little Hans' phobia of horses and Eve White's headaches and blackouts.

Evaluation of the individual differences approach

Strengths
- This approach has important applications, mainly in therapies for treating dysfunctional behaviour. The problem of assessing such therapies is how does one make comparisons? How does one know if someone is 'cured' of depression? Would the person have recovered anyway, without any treatment? How can one ethically conduct research where some people receive a therapy and others do not?

- Case studies give a detailed picture of an individual and help to discover how a person's past may be related to his or her present behaviour.
- By studying unusual behaviour, we can learn more about the usual.

Weaknesses
- The approach may be reductionist because it may overestimate the role of dispositional factors and ignore social and situational influences on behaviour.
- If case study methods are used, the findings can only be applied to the person being studied and not generalised to explain other people's behaviour.
- Retrospective studies may rely on memory, which may be biased or faulty or incomplete, and on past records which may be incomplete.

Item 4   The developmental approach

Developmental psychology focuses on changes that take place in individuals throughout their lifetime, and on trying to explain why they happen.

Development is the sequence of changes that occur over a person's lifetime. Many of the changes are due to inherited factors and maturation (nature). However, a major contribution also comes from the influence of other people and the physical environment (nurture).

There are many aspects to a person's development:
- **cognitive development**, which includes increasing one's knowledge and understanding of the world, and learning language
- **social development**, for example moral development, making friends, and learning pro- and antisocial behaviour
- **personal development**, such as development of the emotional self and self-concepts (for example self-esteem and self-efficacy)

Development continues throughout the lifespan, and there are recognisable phases in development, such as infancy, childhood, adolescence, marriage/becoming a parent, and old age. In each phase, people experience some common changes, and we can examine how these affect their behaviour. For example, in adolescence all children become physically mature, ready to become more independent from their parents and to form attachments outside the family. In old age, there are also common physical changes, as well as issues of independence and relationships with others. At AS, you looked at Piaget's theory of children's cognitive development, and how children's thought processes change with age. The Bandura study looked at the influence of role models to explain the development of social behaviour.

Evaluation of the developmental approach

Strengths
- This approach helps to identify changes that are common to most people and to understand and predict age-related changes in aspects of behaviour. For example, theories of cognitive development can be applied to help improve teaching and learning situations in schools.

- By understanding changes that take place in most people, we can recognise abnormal or dysfunctional development.
- Longitudinal methods can be used to monitor the long-term effect of an experience.

Weaknesses
- If longitudinal research methods are used, it is difficult to control other factors that can also affect what we are measuring, reducing the validity of research conclusions.
- Whether longitudinal or cross-sectional methods are used, large samples are required in order to be able to generalise findings to the research population.
- Longitudinal methods require many participants and researchers, as either may move or withdraw, and these also require long-term funding.
- The developmental approach may be reductionist because it may overestimate the influence of age as a cause of behaviour change and ignore other factors such as social or situational influences on behaviour.

Item 5   The social approach

We spend much of our time with other people, and social psychology focuses on the study of behaviour within a social context, such as family, friends, institutions and culture. Social means involving two or more members of a species, and social behaviour may involve activity within a group or between groups.

We can study the way people interact (social interaction), which includes the influence people have on each other. It is important to remember that social influence can be invisible but that its effects are powerful (such as conformity and obedience).

One of the assumptions of the social approach is that the people we are with (the social situation) have an effect on the way we behave. For example, in the famous Milgram study, it was shown that ordinary American men would follow orders from a perceived legitimate authority, even to the extent that they would give a fatal electric shock to a stranger. Other studies have shown that a person's appearance can shape our expectations and the way we interact with them, and the well-known Rosenhan study showed that behaviour is judged as normal or abnormal depending on the social situation in which it is observed.

Evaluation of the social approach

Strengths
- This approach helps us to focus on the situation in which behaviour is observed, rather than just looking at the characteristics of the person.
- This approach recognises that much behaviour takes place in a social context and helps us to understand how people behave in groups (for example jury decision making).

Weaknesses
- If experimental methods are used, especially laboratory experiments, it is difficult to create an everyday social setting, so research may lack ecological validity (everyday realism).

- Research may be deterministic and may overestimate situational factors and underemphasise the individual differences and the role of 'free will' — but Milgram argued that all his participants could have refused to administer electric shocks.

Item 6   The behaviourist perspective

Behaviourist psychology assumes that all behaviour is learned, and that experience and interaction with the environment make us what we are because we learn stimulus–response units of behaviour in reaction to the environment. This perspective has been called **environmental determinism**, because behaviour is determined by past experience.

- **Radical behaviourism** takes the view that all behaviour is learned, but nowadays most behaviourists take a less radical view.
- **Neo-behaviourism** is an extension of behaviourism. The best-known example is **social learning theory**, which was an attempt by Albert Bandura to reformulate learning theory to include a role for cognitive factors such as perception, attention and memory.

Assumptions of the behaviourist perspective

- Humans and non-human animals are only quantitatively different. This is supported by the theory of evolution, which suggests that all animals have evolved from a common ancestor and are 'built' from the same stimulus–response units. This means that behaviourists can generalise from research on non-human animals (such as rats and pigeons) to human behaviour.
- There is no need to look at what goes on inside the 'black box' of the mind (for example perception, attention, language, memory, thinking and so on); psychologists need only be concerned with external and observable behaviour.
- All behaviour can be explained in terms of conditioning theory through classical and/or operant conditioning to produce stimulus and response (S–R) links, which build up to produce more complex behaviours.
- All behaviour is determined by environmental influences, i.e. learning. We are born as a blank slate upon which stimulus–response (S–R) units are built. This is environmental determinism.

Evaluation of behaviourism

Strengths
- Classic learning theory has had a major influence on all branches of psychology.
- Behaviourism has given rise to many practical applications, such as treatments for dysfunctional behaviour, where desirable behaviours are rewarded. The principle is that if dysfunctional behaviour (such as a phobia) is learned, then it can be unlearned.

Weaknesses
- It is a mechanistic (machine-like) perspective, which ignores consciousness, subjective experience and emotions. We are 'puppets' on the strings of our past experience.
- It excludes the role of cognitive (mental) factors (except for social learning theory).
- It denies the role of innate factors.

- It is deterministic: behaviour is determined by the environment and by past experience. It implies that humans are passive in response to their environment.
- It is reductionist: it reduces complex behaviour to stimulus–response links.
- It is largely based on work with non-human animals. However, behaviourists argue that the theory of evolution shows that human and non-human animals are quantitatively not qualitatively different, and therefore such research is meaningful.
- The use of behaviourist learning programmes to control others (as in some prisons and psychiatric institutions using reward and punishment) could be considered unethical.

Item 7   The psychodynamic perspective

The psychodynamic perspective, whose founding father was Sigmund Freud, explains human behaviour in terms of an interaction between innate drives and early experience.

Freud wrote that there are three parts to the human psyche (personality):

- The **id** is the primitive, innate part of personality.
- The **ego** is the conscious and intellectual part of personality that regulates the id.
- The **superego** is the moral part that is learned from parents and society.

These parts are hypothetical entities (they do not actually exist) and they develop through the five psychosexual stages: oral, anal, phallic, latent and genital.

Assumptions of the psychodynamic perspective

- Human development is a dynamic process and early experience drives us to behave in predictable ways.
- Childhood is a critical period of development. Infants are born with innate biological drives, for example for oral satisfaction, and these drives have a physical (sexual) basis. If these drives are not satisfied, this can lead to personality or behavioural problems later in life.
- If these drives are not satisfied, the ego copes by using ego-defence mechanisms, for example repression and denial, and thoughts, feelings and behaviour can be influenced as a result.
- Individual personality differences can be traced back to the way early conflicts were handled in infancy and childhood, and these conflicts remain with the adult and exert pressure through unconsciously motivated behaviour.

Evaluation of the psychodynamic perspective

Strengths

- Freud recognised that childhood is a critical period of development.
- The theory has been enormously influential within psychology, and beyond.
- This approach focuses on the individual rather than on general laws of behaviour. Psychodynamic theory provides a rich picture of individual personality.

Weaknesses

- The theory lacks empirical support (objective research evidence), and where there is 'evidence', this is mostly from case studies of middle-class, European women, many of whom experienced anxiety disorders.

- The data were collected retrospectively, and because it was interpreted there is the potential for investigator bias. Also, Freud may have influenced the things his patients said (case study of Little Hans).
- It reduces human activity to a basic set of abstract concepts (id, ego, superego), which are presented as if they are real things.
- It is deterministic, because it implies that people have little free will, and it suggests that adult behaviour is determined by childhood experiences.

Questions

1 Read Items 1–7.

a List *three* psychological studies that take the physiological approach to explain human behaviour.

b Outline *two* assumptions from the physiological approach.

c Describe *one* study that supports the physiological approach in psychology.

d Suggest *two* advantages of using the physiological approach to explain human behaviour.

....

....

....

....

....

e Suggest *one* disadvantage of using the physiological approach to explain human behaviour.

....

....

....

f Explain why physiological explanations of human behaviour may be described as reductionist.

....

....

....

....

g Select *one* other approach in psychology (such as cognitive) and suggest in what way this differs from the physiological approach.

....

....

....

....

....

....

....

....

2 Read Items 1–7.

a List *three* psychological studies that take the cognitive approach to explain human behaviour

....

....

....

b Outline *two* assumptions from the cognitive approach.

....

....

....

....

....

c Describe *one* study that supports the cognitive approach in psychology.

....

....

....

....

....

....

....

....

d Suggest *two* advantages of using the cognitive approach to explain human behaviour.

....

....

....

....

....

....

e Suggest *one* disadvantage of using the cognitive approach to explain human behaviour.

....

....

....

....

....

f Select *one* other approach in psychology (such as psychodynamic) and suggest in what way this differs from the cognitive approach.

....

....

....

....

....

....

3 Read Items 1–7.

a List *three* psychological studies that take the individual differences approach to explain human behaviour.

....

....

....

b Outline the assumption from the individual differences approach.

....

....

....

....

....

c Describe *one* study that supports the individual differences approach in psychology.

....

....

....

....

....

....

....

d Suggest *one* advantage of using the individual differences approach to explain human behaviour.

....

....

....

....

e Suggest *one* disadvantage of using the individual differences approach to explain human behaviour.

....

....

....

....

f Select *one* other approach in psychology (such as physiological) and suggest in what way this differs from the individual differences approach.

....

....

....

....

....

....

....

4 Read Items 1–7.

a List *three* psychological studies that take the developmental approach to explain human behaviour.

....

....

....

b Outline *two* assumptions from the developmental approach.

....

....

....

....

....

c Describe *one* study that supports the developmental approach in psychology.

....

....

....

....

....

....

....

....

d Suggest *one* advantage of using the developmental approach to explain human behaviour.

....

....

....

....

e Suggest *one* disadvantage of using the developmental approach to explain human behaviour.

....

....

....

....

f Psychologists who take a developmental approach may use longitudinal research methods. Explain *two* of the problems faced by psychologists who conduct longitudinal research.

....

....

....

....

....

5 Read Items 1–7.

a List *three* psychological studies that take the social approach to explain human behaviour.

....

....

....

b Outline the assumptions of the social approach.

....

....

....

....

c Describe *one* study that supports the social approach in psychology.

....

....

(Continued overleaf)

....

....

d Suggest *one* advantage of using the social approach to explain human behaviour.

....

e Suggest *one* disadvantage of using the social approach to explain human behaviour.

....

f Psychologists who take a social approach may use experimental research methods. Explain *one* problem faced by psychologists who conduct experimental research to explain social behaviour.

....

6 Read Items 1–7.

a List *three* psychological studies that explain human behaviour from the behaviourist perspective.

....

b Outline *two* assumptions from the behaviourist perspective.

....

....

....

....

....

....

c Describe *one* study that explains behaviour from a behaviourist perspective.

....

....

....

....

....

....

....

....

....

....

....

....

d Suggest *one* advantage of using the behaviourist perspective to explain human behaviour.

....

....

....

....

....

....

e Suggest *one* disadvantage of using the behaviourist perspective to explain human behaviour.

....

....

....

....

f Explain why research from the behaviourist perspective may be described as deterministic.

....

....

....

....

....

g Select *one* other approach in psychology (such as physiological) and suggest in what way this differs from the behaviourist perspective.

....

....

....

....

....

....

....

....

7 Read Items 1–7.

a List *two* psychological studies that explain human behaviour from the psychodynamic perspective.

....

....

....

b Outline *two* assumptions from the psychodynamic perspective.

....

....

....

....

....

c Describe *one* study that explains behaviour from a psychodynamic perspective.

....

....

....

....

....

....

....

....

d Suggest *one* advantage of using the psychodynamic perspective to explain human behaviour.

....

....

....

....

e Suggest *two* disadvantages of using the psychodynamic perspective to explain human behaviour.

....

....

....

....

....

....

f Explain why research from the psychodynamic perspective may be described as deterministic.

....

....

....

....

....

....

g Select *one* other approach in psychology (such as behaviourist) and compare and contrast this with the psychodynamic perspective.

Hint: 'Compare and contrast' requires you to explain in which ways the two perspectives are similar and in which ways they differ. Use a separate sheet of paper and write about 200 words.

Approaches, perspectives, issues and debates

Topic 2   Issues and debates

A debate is discussion involving the consideration of different sides of a question. Some debates within psychology are:

- free will vs determinism
- nature vs nurture
- reductionism vs holism
- ethnocentrism
- psychology as a science

Item 1   Free will vs determinism

Most people feel that they have free will to make choices that are not determined for them and are the product of their own volition. However, this position creates difficulties for scientific research, which assumes deterministic relationships. Determinism suggests that individuals cannot be held morally responsible for their actions.

Where do the approaches and perspectives stand on this debate?

Physiological approach: this usually sees behaviour as being caused by biological factors, and if this is the case then behaviour is determined by biology, so the individual has no free will to choose to behave differently.

Cognitive approach: this explains behaviour as being caused by cognitive factors, for example thought processes, attention and decision making. Thus this approach does allow free will to choose behaviour. For example, in cognitive behavioural therapy it is assumed that the person can choose not to think irrationally.

Individual differences: this often looks at the behaviour of one person and whether the resulting case study allows 'free will' may depend on which approach/perspective is used. For example, Thigpen and Cleckley looked at Eve's behaviour from the psychodynamic perspective.

Developmental approach: this may explain behaviour as being caused by maturation (ageing), in which case behaviour is determined by biology, so the individual has no free will to choose to behave differently. For example, Piaget suggests that children's thought processes change at predetermined ages, thus giving a deterministic explanation.

Social approach: this looks at the behaviour of people in groups. Whether the research allows 'free will' may depend on which approach/perspective is used. For example, Milgram maintained that although his participants were influenced by the social situation they were in, they had the free will to choose not to continue giving electric shocks.

Behaviourist perspective: this usually explains behaviour in terms of stimulus–response learning caused by past experience, and if this is the case then the individual has no free will to choose to behave differently, because behaviour is determined by past experiences.

Psychodynamic perspective: this explains behaviour in terms of unconscious forces that the individual can neither escape nor explain. In addition, because the unconscious forces are the result of early childhood experience, behaviour is determined by two factors — by the past and by unconscious motivation — so the individual has no free will to choose his or her behaviour.

Item 2   Nature vs nurture

To what extent is any behaviour the result of your genetic code (nature — the genes you inherit) or due to your life experiences (nurture — your parents, your upbringing, your experiences generally)? This is a continuing debate, especially in the areas of language, aggression, gender and dysfunctional behaviour. Of course, nature and nurture interact, and much research sees nature as 'potential' that is modified by nurture.

Where do the approaches and perspectives stand on this debate?

Physiological approach: some research suggests that behaviour is caused by biological factors, and if this is the case then behaviour is caused by nature. However, the research by Maguire found that the hippocampus in the brains of taxi drivers changed as a result of their environment, which suggests an interaction between nature and nurture.

Cognitive approach: an example of the nature–nurture debate in cognitive psychology is the question of how children acquire the ability to use human language. On the nature side of the argument is Noam Chomsky, who proposes that we are born with an innate, biological, language acquisition device that facilitates, during a critical period, the development of language. On the nurture side of the argument are the behaviourists, especially B. F. Skinner, who propose that we learn to use human language by imitation and reinforcement. Many attempts to teach non-human primates to communicate using human language, such as the Gardner and Gardner case study of Washoe, and the Savage Rumbaugh study of Kanzi, have not given a definite answer to this question.

Developmental approach: some research explains behaviour as being caused by nature (ageing), in which case behaviour is determined by nature; for example, Piaget suggests that children's thought processes change at predetermined ages. However, the developmental approach does not always take the nature side of the debate; for example, Bandura demonstrated that aggressive behaviour is not innate, and that children who observe adult role models behaving aggressively learn from what they see and imitate aggressive actions.

Social approach: much social research takes the nurture side of the debate, showing that behaviour is influenced by the social environment. For example, research by Piliavin et al. demonstrated that it was not the dispositional characteristics of the passengers, for example their kind nature, but the situation of the victim (lame or drunk) that influenced whether help was given.

Behaviourist perspective: this explains behaviour in terms of nurture. From the perspective of behaviourists, when we are born we are a 'blank slate' and from the moment of birth we learn our behaviour.

Psychodynamic perspective: this recognises the influence of both nature and nurture. According to Freud, the id is the innate (nature) part of the human personality, driving us to seek pleasure and avoid pain, but the ego and superego are developed as a result of early experiences (nurture).

Item 3   Reductionism vs holism

Reductionism is the principle of analysing complex things into simple constituents or the use of simple principles, for example explaining complex human behaviour in terms of simplistic single-factor causes, such as inherited genes.

Holism is the principle that complex phenomena cannot be understood through an analysis of the constituent parts alone, because the behaviour of the whole system cannot be explained in terms of the 'sum' of the behaviour of all of the different parts.

Reductionism is a goal of science, but although simple explanations are appropriate in some situations, they rarely explain the richness of human experience and prevent the search for more complex answers.

Where do the approaches and perspectives stand on this debate?

Many psychological accounts that are determinist are also reductionist.

Physiological approach: physiological reductionism explains behaviour in terms of biological factors (especially in terms of genes, as in some explanations of dysfunctional behaviour).

Cognitive approach: this can be described as reductionist when it proposes a computer-like information processing approach as a means to describe and explain behaviour.

Behaviourist perspective: this uses a reductionist vocabulary: stimulus, response, reinforcement and punishment. This is called environmental reductionism because behaviourists reduce the concept of the mind to behavioural components, i.e. stimulus–response links.

Psychodynamic perspective: this is reductionist because it relies on the interaction between three components, the id, ego and superego, to explain complex behaviour.

Evaluation of reductionism

- One of the basic goals of science is to reduce all phenomena to separate simple parts in order to understand how they work, so reductionism may be a necessary part of understanding what causes human behaviour.
- Reductionist hypotheses are easier to test, and the fact that they can be 'proven' (or not) makes them more believable.
- Reductionist explanations distract psychologists because simple explanations for behaviour prevent further attempts to find more complex but less clear-cut explanations.

Item 4   Ethnocentrism

Ethnocentrism refers to the tendency of people to view the world from their own particular cultural or social group. This often leads to overestimating the importance and 'normality' of people who are in one cultural group and to underestimating the importance, worth and 'normality' of people who are not in that group.

When psychological research findings are based on a culturally biased sample of people, but are then applied to explain the behaviour of people from another culture, the research can be criticised as being ethnocentric. In order to gain a full understanding of human behaviour, it is necessary to understand the cultures in which people live.

One way to overcome ethnocentric bias is to undertake cross-cultural research, because this allows us to compare groups of people who have been brought up in different cultures, for example different social or ethnic backgrounds. Cross-cultural research has advantages and disadvantages.

Advantages of cross-cultural research

- Identifying characteristics and/or behaviour that seem to be universal provides informed evidence for the nature–nurture debate.
- Highlighting the differences between cultures helps us challenge our own assumptions as to what is good/bad or normal/abnormal.

Disadvantages of cross-cultural research

- Cross-cultural studies are expensive and time consuming, and can be used to suggest that one culture is superior or 'normal'.
- No researcher can escape from the fact that he or she interprets events through the 'schema' of his or her own culture.
- Questions may be understood differently by individuals from different cultures.
- Cross-cultural studies are only a sample of that culture and may not be generalisable.

Item 5   Is psychology a science?

Science is a continuing effort to discover and increase human knowledge and understanding through disciplined research. Using controlled methods, scientists collect observable evidence, record measurable data relating to the observations, and analyse this information to construct theoretical explanations of how things work.

The methods of scientific research include the generation of hypotheses and experimentation to test these hypotheses under controlled conditions. Scientists are also expected to publish their information, so that other scientists can carry out similar experiments to check the reliability of their conclusions. The results of this process enable better understanding of past events and a better ability to predict future events of the same kind as those that have been tested.

The scientific method involves:
- setting up an alternative hypothesis
- operationalising the IV and DV (so the study can be repeated to verify reliability)

- collecting quantitative data under controlled conditions
- objectively analysing the data in the light of the hypothesis
- accepting or rejecting the alternative hypothesis
- establishing a general law/theory for which evidence can be collected by scientific methods

Psychology is a science, but some people do not think it can ever be an objective science and ask whether experimental methods are appropriate to psychology.

Questions

1 Read Items 1–5.

a Explain what is meant by the terms 'determinism' and 'free will'.

....

....

....

....

....

....

....

b Explain why *one* of the approaches/perspectives proposes a deterministic explanation of human behaviour.

....

....

....

....

....

....

....

c Suggest *one* advantage and *one* disadvantage of taking a determinist approach to explain human behaviour.

....

....

(Continued overleaf)

....

....
....
....
....
....
....
....

2 Read Items 1–5.

a Explain what is meant by the terms 'nature' and 'nurture'.

....
....
....
....
....

b Explain why *one* of the approaches/perspectives gives a 'nature' explanation of human behaviour.

....
....
....
....
....
....

c Explain why *one* of the approaches/perspectives gives a 'nurture' explanation of human behaviour.

....
....
....
....

....

....

....

d Suggest *one* advantage and *one* disadvantage of explaining human behaviour from the 'nature' approach.

....

....

....

....

....

....

....

....

e Suggest *one* advantage and *one* disadvantage of explaining human behaviour from the 'nurture' approach.

....

....

....

....

....

....

....

....

3 *Exam-style question*

Discuss, using evidence, the nature–nurture debate in psychology.

Hint: Make a plan for this essay and write four paragraphs. In each paragraph, argue, based on evidence, a different point related to nature or nurture. Each paragraph should contain:
- the approach
- an example
- research evidence for nature
- research evidence for nurture
- evidence of interaction between nature and nurture, or evaluative comment

Do not forget to end with an appropriate conclusion.

When you have completed the plan, write your essay on a separate piece of paper and ask your teacher to assess your work.

....

....

....

....

....

....

....

....

....

....

....

....

....

....

....

4 Read Items 1–5.

a Explain what is meant by the terms 'reductionism' and 'holism'.

....

....

....

....

....

....

b Suggest *one* research study that gives a reductionist explanation of human behaviour and explain why this study is reductionist.

....

....

....

....

....

....

....

....

c Explain why *one* of the approaches/perspectives gives a reductionist interpretation of human behaviour.

....

....

....

....

....

....

d Explain *one* advantage and *one* disadvantage of explaining human behaviour in reductionist terms.

....

....

....

....

....

....

....

5 *Exam-style question*

Discuss, using evidence, the reductionism–holism debate in psychology.

Hint: Make a plan for this essay and write four paragraphs. In each paragraph, argue, based on evidence, a different point related to reductionism or holism. Each paragraph should include:
- the approach
- an example
- research evidence for reductionism
- research evidence or argument for holism
- evaluative comment

Do not forget to end with an appropriate conclusion.

When you have completed the plan, write your essay on a separate piece of paper and ask your teacher to assess your work.

6 Read Items 1–5.

a Explain what is meant by the term 'ethnocentric'.

b Explain why the conclusions of psychological research findings could be ethnocentric.

c Outline *one* psychological research study whose conclusions may be culturally biased.

d Suggest *one* advantage and *one* disadvantage of conducting cross-cultural research.

....

....

....

....

....

....

7 Read Items 1–5.

a Outline *three* features of the scientific method.

....

....

....

....

b Suggest *one* advantage of using the scientific method in psychology.

....

....

....

....

....

c Suggest *one* disadvantage of using the scientific method in psychology.

....

....

....

....

....

d Discuss how scientific methods increase our understanding of everyday life.

Hint: the key words in this question are 'discuss', 'scientific methods' and 'everyday life'. An effective discussion should be a two-sided argument supported by evidence. 'Scientific methods' can be summarised as experimental methodologies (for example laboratory, field and natural experiments) that collect quantitative data.

Make a plan for this essay and write four paragraphs. In each paragraph, argue a different point, supported by evidence, explaining how scientific methods (experimental methods) have increased our understanding of 'everyday life'. Balance your discussion by arguing the limitations of using scientific methodologies to explain 'everyday life'. When you have completed the plan, write your essay and ask your teacher to assess it. You could work with another student to develop this essay.